First Spelling

5–7 years

Notes for grown-ups

- This book has been written to help your child develop their first spelling skills. They will practise spelling words in different contexts and learn about vowels, syllables, homophones, plurals, silent letters and more.

- The activities in this book are organized to build on what your child learned on the previous page. If they are finding something tricky, go back to a page they feel confident with.

- Some of the activities in this book require additional learning materials. You will need some coloured pencils or crayons.

- Left-handed children should tilt the book so that the top left corner is higher than the right. The book should be slightly to the left of their bodies. This will help them to see their writing and avoid smudging.

- Look out for the **How are you doing?** sections. These give your child an opportunity to reflect on their progress and give you an idea of how your child is doing.

- Let your child check their own answers at the back of the book. Encourage them to talk about what they have learned.

Educational Consultant: Claire Hubbard.
With thanks to Child Autism UK, Pace, Amy Callaby and Jack Callaby.

Your Ladybird Class friends!

Zara Penguin loves all kinds of dance, as well as stories about princesses, knights and superheroes. Zara has cerebral palsy and wears an ankle-foot orthosis on each leg to help her walk. Her favourite lessons are history and circle time.

Nia Hedgehog is the newest member of Ladybird Class! She loves video games and skateboarding. Her favourite lessons are computing and geography.

Tao Meerkat wants to save the planet! He loves animals, nature and the environment. But he also likes magical stories and role-playing. His favourite lessons are science and phonics.

Olivia Crocodile always has lots of energy and is ready to change the world! She loves building things, and she has a red belt in karate. Her favourite lessons are maths and PE.

Noah Panda loves to craft, play on the computer and, most of all, he loves to bake. He collects lots of things like badges and pebbles. Noah is on the autism spectrum. His favourite lessons are art and playtime.

Ali Lion is quiet, but his head is full of daydreams and imagination. He loves to sing and to dress up in fancy costumes. His favourite lessons are literacy and music.

Contents

Letters games

Ladybird Class are learning letters and the sound that each letter makes.

There are 26 letters in the alphabet. 5 letters are **vowels** and 21 letters are **consonants**. The orange letters at the bottom of the page are the vowels and the yellow letters are the consonants.

Find the vowels

Ali Lion is counting the vowels in his friends' names. Circle the vowels with your favourite pencil.

Ali   Noah

Tao   Zara

Olivia   Nia

How many different vowels are in your name? Write it out on a piece of paper and circle them!

Missing vowels

Can you add the vowels to complete the words?

 m_lk

 j_mp

 s_ndp_t

 w_ndm_ll

 p_nd

 s_ndw_ch

 l_nchb_x

 sp_ _n

 tr_ _

 sw_ng

a b c d e f g h i j k l m

Vowel swap

Try swapping the vowels in the words below and see what new words you can make.

I can make different words with different vowels. If I swap the **a** in "cat" for the letter **u**, I get the word "cut"!

bell _____

bond _____

sock _____

Mix and match the sounds

Look at the pictures and say the words out loud. Fill in the consonants that complete Olivia Crocodile's words.

 ___ a ___

 ___ o ___ ey

 ___ o ___

 ___ o ___

 ___ ai ___

 ___ a ___ o ___

Did you know the letter **y** acts as a vowel sometimes? Like in the words "baby" and "fly".

| n | o | p | q | r | s | t | u | v | w | x | y | z |

Tidy digraphs

Nia Hedgehog has been learning about digraphs while tidying her bedroom. Can you help?

A **digraph** is a two-letter sound, like **ch**, **sh**, **ee** and **ow**. A digraph can be made up of two vowels or two consonants, or one of each.

Nia Hedgehog needs to put away all the things that have a digraph. Help her by using the digraphs to fill in the missing letters. Tick the objects once you have found them in Nia's bedroom.

ch	oo
sh	ar
th	or
ai	oy
ee	ow
oa	oi

b_____ ☐

pill_____ ☐

____air ☐

t_____ ☐

b____k ☐

gr_____n ☐

c____s ☐

f____k ☐

bru____ ☐

c_____ns ☐

6

t __ el

b __ t

clo __ es

tr __ n

slo __

Have a look in your own bedroom! What things do you have that might be spelled with digraphs?

Digraph disco

Ladybird Class are at the school disco. They are learning more digraphs today. Time to get your dancing shoes on!

Do the digraph dance

Olivia Crocodile is teaching Ali Lion and Zara Penguin some new dances. She's even drawn out the steps on the floor so they don't trip over their feet! Fill out the words in each step so that everyone can get dancing!

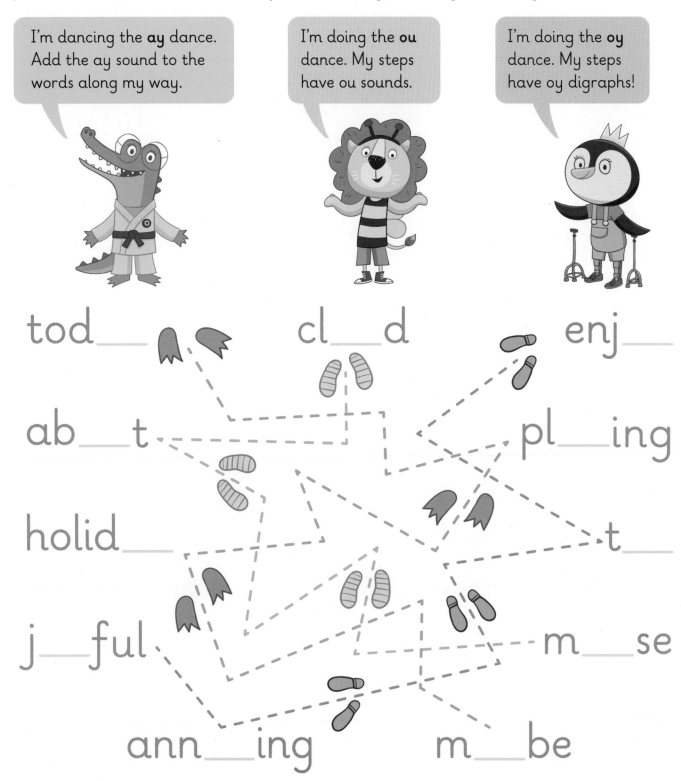

I'm dancing the **ay** dance. Add the ay sound to the words along my way.

I'm doing the **ou** dance. My steps have ou sounds.

I'm doing the **oy** dance. My steps have oy digraphs!

tod___

cl__d

enj___

ab__t

pl__ing

holid___

_t__

j__ful

m__se

ann__ing

m__be

Doubling up

Ladybird Class are dancing in pairs, just like digraphs that are made up of a pair of letters. Can you help them find the rhythm by colouring matching sounds in the same colours? The sounds are:

ie	ea	ir	ue	aw	ew	oe

tie   draw   blue   mangoes

new   yawn   toe   magpie

feast   girl   least   clue

shirt   saw   dawn   beast

straw   east   whirl   fawn

grew   true   third   lie

Digraphs and trigraphs

Ladybird Class are trying to find the missing letters for these words. They are learning about split digraphs and trigraphs.

Split digraphs

The split digraphs are missing in the recipe. Fill them in using the split digraphs in the panel.

A **split digraph** is a two-letter sound that is split up by another letter. The split digraphs are:

a_e as in "bake"
e_e as in "theme"
i_e as in "time"
o_e as in "hope"
u_e as in "tune" or "rude"

You will need:

- Plenty of t __ m __

- 20 c __ b __ s of sugar

- Flour to sh __ k __ into the mix

- Qu __ t __ a lot of butter

- 2 eggs that you br __ k __ earlier

- A paper c __ n __ to __ c __ the cupc __ k __ s

Instructions

1 Mix together then b __ k __ it in the oven.

2 Decor __ t __ it on a pl __ t __

with a sugar r __ s __ and

a chocolate fl __ k __ .

*Recipe for illustrative purposes only

Trigraphs

Ladybird Class are learning about trigraphs.
Guess the words and write them under the pictures.

> A **trigraph** is a three-letter sound, like **igh**, **ear**, **air** and **ure**.

igh

ear

air

ure

How are you doing?

Did you enjoy learning about split digraphs and trigraphs?

☐ Yes, I know some split digraphs and trigraphs.
☐ I almost get it, but I need more practice with them.

Words with rhythm

It's time for a singalong! Let's make some noise and dance to the beat because today we're learning about syllables.

Syllables are how many "beats" are in a word. Try saying these words and clap your hands together for each sound.

CLAP!

CLATTER!

HONK!

How many times did you clap for each word?

"Clap" and "honk" each have one syllable, and "clatter" has two syllables.

Clap out the syllables or "beats" as you say each word below.
Count the claps and write the number.

	syllable(s)		syllable(s)
recorder	___	rattle	___
drum	___	violin	___
singing	___	trumpet	___
music	___	horn	___
instrument	___	piano	___

Can you help Ladybird Class tidy everything up for the day?
Match each picture to a word.

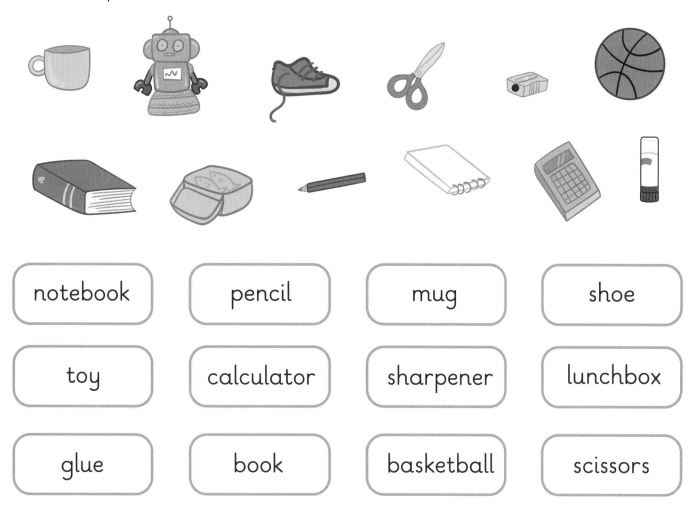

notebook	pencil	mug	shoe
toy	calculator	sharpener	lunchbox
glue	book	basketball	scissors

How many syllables does each word have? Write the word in the correct box.

1 syllable	2 syllables
3 syllables	**More than 3 syllables**

Same but different

The friends in Ladybird Class are learning about homophones. Can you help?

Homophone snap

Match the words and pictures that sound the same by drawing a line between them.

There are lots of words that sound the same but are written differently and mean different things. These words are called **homophones**.

blue

knight

brake

flour

hair

sea

flower

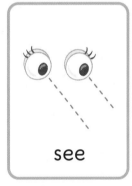

see

bear

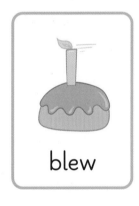

blew

break

bare

night

hare

Make your own set of homophone cards and play snap! How many homophones can you think of?

The playscript

Tao Meerkat and Nia Hedgehog are writing a play to perform for Ladybird Class! But they are getting some homophones mixed up. Circle the correct word to complete their script.

Tao: So nice to **meat** / **meet** you today.

Nia: Well, I've **missed** / **mist** hanging out with you.

Tao: **Where** / **Wear** are we going?

Nia: We're going to the beach by the **sea** / **see**.

Tao: What will we do when we get **there** / **their**?

Nia: We need to ask the **witch** / **which** for help!

Tao: Do you **know** / **no** which way to go?

Nia: I do! We need to turn **right** / **write**!

Flower-sound families

Ladybird Class are watering some flowers in the community garden. They are listening for sounds that are said in the same way but are spelled differently.

Read the words underneath the flowers. Listen for the sounds. Then colour each flower to match the watering can with the same sound.

I will water the flowers that have the **ai** sound, like in "rain" and "plane".

My flowers have **ie** sounds, like in "tie" and "fly".

I will water the **ee** sounds, like in "leek" and "tweak".

My flowers have **oo** sounds, like in "spoon" and "June".

I need to find flowers with **oa** sounds, like in "coat" and "blow".

My flowers have **ow** sounds, like in "owl" and "cloud".

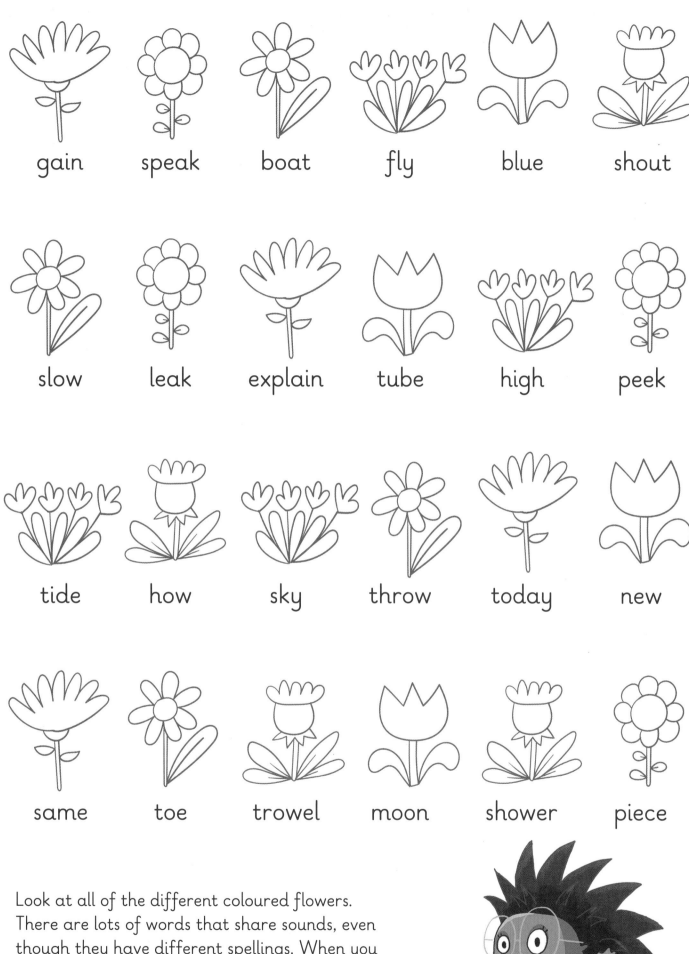

gain speak boat fly blue shout

slow leak explain tube high peek

tide how sky throw today new

same toe trowel moon shower piece

Look at all of the different coloured flowers.
There are lots of words that share sounds, even
though they have different spellings. When you
group them together, they make sound families.

Sneaky spellings

Ladybird Class are looking for all the words with sneaky spellings. These words sound different to how they are spelled.

Silent letters

Noah Panda and Zara Penguin are trying to be as quiet as possible, just like silent letters! Circle the letters in the words that don't make any sound.

Silent letters don't make any sound when you say the word. They are super-sneaky!

whale

autumn

answer

comb

ghost

Read each word aloud slowly. Which letter can't you hear?

scissors

island

18

Sounds like

These words have been written the way they sound, but that's not how they are spelled. Write out the correct spellings.

Sometimes I spell "fable" wrong because the **le** at the end sounds like **ul**, like "fabul".

tabul   sed   haz

whith   luv   tryd   shoogar

Looks like

Some words look like they should be correct but they are not.
Look at each picture and cross out the two incorrect spellings.

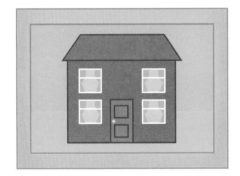

hows
howse
house

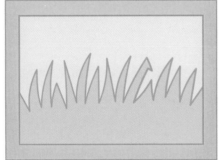

gras
grass
grase

frends
freinds
friends

i
eye
ai

farver
father
further

Keep a record of spellings that you find tricky. You can look at them and practise writing them.

Gone fishing

Ladybird Class have gone fishing for the day. They are going to learn about some special letters and sounds.

Help Ali Lion and Tao Meerkat catch the fish! Fill in the missing letters **nk** or **tion** to complete the words.

The **nk** sound comes after a vowel sound, and **tion** usually goes at the end of the word.

dri_____   na_____

thi_____   pi_____

si_____ing   mo_____ey

tha_____s   li_____

educa_____   competi_____

subtrac_____   addi_____

New endings

Add **tch**, **dge**, or **ge** next to the letters below to complete the words. Remember, some have more than one answer.

> The **tch** and **dge** sounds come after short vowel sounds, but **ge** comes after all other sounds at the end of the word.

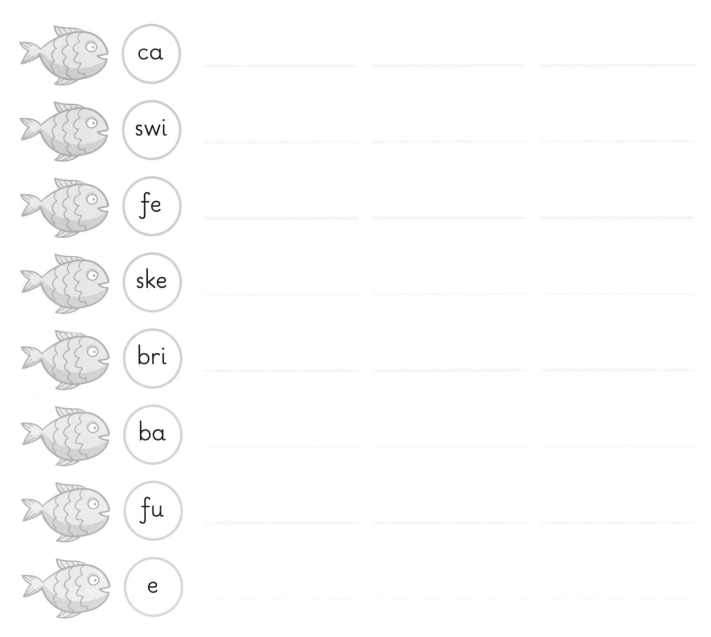

ca

swi

fe

ske

bri

ba

fu

e

Home time

Tao Meerkat and Ali Lion put all the fish back in the water.
Look at the fish. If the word is spelled wrong, colour it in.

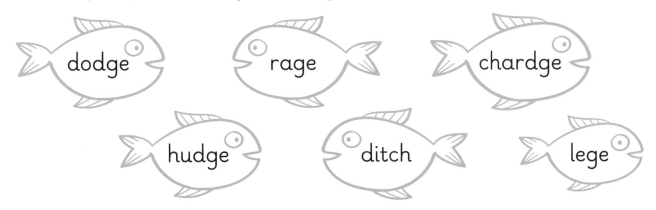

dodge

rage

chardge

hudge

ditch

lege

Forest plurals

Ladybird Class are taking a trip to the forest. They are looking for lots of objects that they can turn into plurals.

When there is one of something, it is called a **singular**. When there is more than one, it is a **plural**. Often, the plural of a word has **s** at the end. For example, the plural of "tree" is "trees".

Collecting objects

Ladybird Class are making piles of things that belong in the forest and things that don't. Write the correct plurals below, then circle the things that shouldn't be in the forest.

 can ___

feather ___

crisp packet ___

twig ___

 plastic bag ___

 pine cone ___

 sweet wrapper ___

 acorn ___

cap ___

mushroom ___

 bottle ___

Funny plurals

The friends are making a secret den! Write the correct plural for the things in their camp.

Sometimes, words ending in certain letters need to be pluralized differently. Words that end in **sh, ch, ss, s, x** or **z** need **es** to become a plural.

Hmm. What's the plural for a bush?

One bush, two bushes!

The **es** plural always sounds like **iz**!

blanket

torch

glass

flag

lunchbox

robin

apple

bench

umbrella

How are you doing?

How are you feeling about plurals?

Good, I understand these plurals.

I'm starting to get it, but I need some help.

Practising prefixes

Ladybird Class are building new words by adding groups of letters called prefixes. Join in!

Noah Panda and Olivia Crocodile are building loads of excellent bridges. They are adding the prefix **un-** to create new words. Can you help?

Prefixes go at the front of other groups of letters. Adding a prefix changes the meaning of the word.

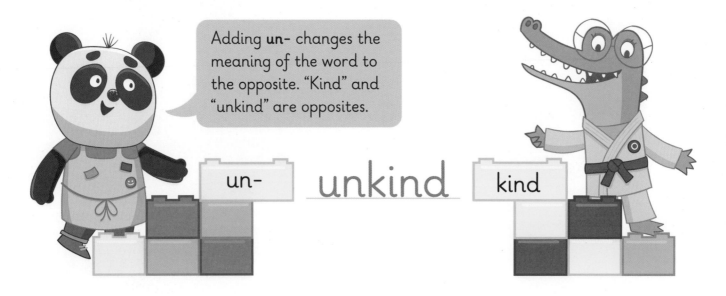

Adding **un-** changes the meaning of the word to the opposite. "Kind" and "unkind" are opposites.

un-   unkind   kind

Can you write out the new words to connect the bridges together?

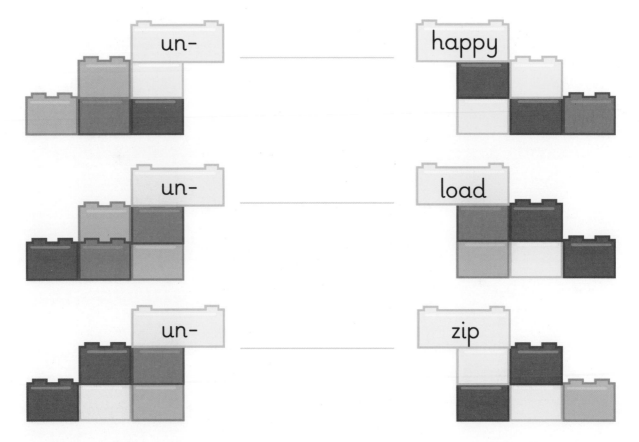

un- _____ happy

un- _____ load

un- _____ zip

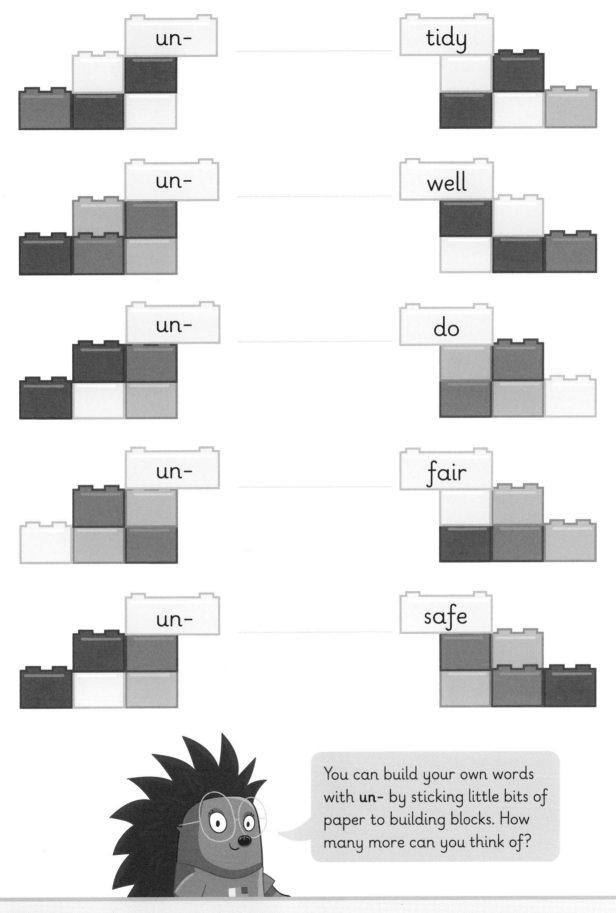

un-   tidy

un-   well

un-   do

un-   fair

un-   safe

You can build your own words with **un-** by sticking little bits of paper to building blocks. How many more can you think of?

How are you doing?

How do you feel about learning the prefix **un-**?

- [ ] Great! I like using the prefix **un-** to build new words.
- [ ] I could use a bit more help, please.

Suffix games

Ali Lion and Zara Penguin are playing a video game. They are making new words with suffixes!

-ment, -ness, -less and -ful

Zara Penguin has to go through a maze! Follow the dotted lines to make new words using suffixes. Then write the words in the boxes. Give it a try!

end
care
ill
move
pave
joy
fit
fear
good
wonder
use
agree

_____ment	_____ful
_____ment	_____ful
_____ment	_____ful

_____less	_____ness
_____less	_____ness
_____less	_____ness

-ly and -ing

Choose the correct suffix from **-ly** and **-ing** for these words, then write the new word.

> When you are adding **-ing** to a word that ends in a vowel, you replace the vowel with the **i** of **ing**. Like this: "make" becomes "making".

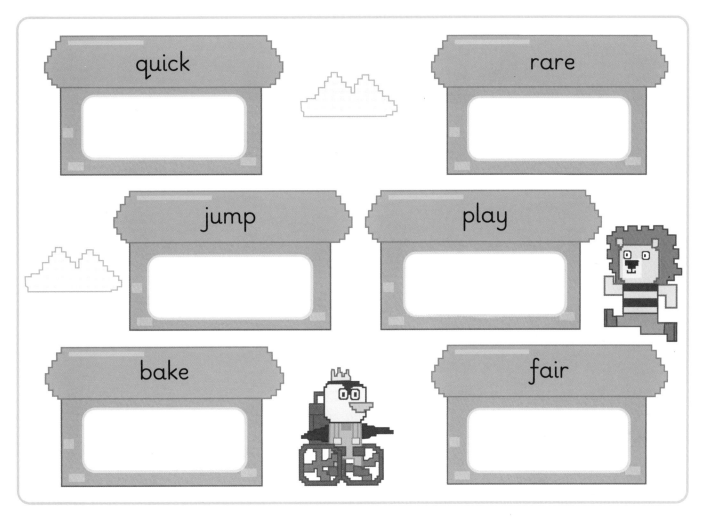

quick

rare

jump

play

bake

fair

-er and -est

Woohoo! Final level! Add the suffixes **-er** and **-est** to these words to create new words.

> We can add **-er** or **-est** at the end of words to show when there is more of something or the most of something. Like "loud", "louder", "LOUDEST"!

fast

slow

small

tall

Collecting words

Ladybird Class love collecting different things. Today they are collecting compound words.

By putting two words together, you can sometimes make a new word. These are called **compound** words.

Let's make some compound words! Choose a word from the box and add it to the end of a word below. Try it with all of the words. Remember, you can only use each word once.

shake   fly   brush   ground   day

birth_____

paint_____

milk_____

dragon_____

play_____

Football has "foot" and "ball" next to each other!

"Football" is a compound word because you use your foot to kick the ball. Can you guess why other compound words are put together?

Sticking words back together

Oh dear! Zara Penguin's book was accidentally ripped. Draw lines between the ripped words to make some compound words.

bow

fly

pop

space

corn

ship

skate

butter

board

rain

Make up your own compound words by putting your favourite words together.

How are you doing?

How do you feel about spotting compound words?

☐ I'm ready to teach someone else!
☐ I could use a bit more help.

Spelling champion!

Ladybird Class have had so much fun learning how to spell with you! Now it's time to show them what you've learned. You've got this!

Have a look at the words on the whiteboards.
Circle the correct spelling in each group.

fast   fasd   farst

worter   warter   water

munny   money   monee

Don't forget, you can always ask for help!

thanks   fanks   thanx

skool   scool   school

yoo   you   yue

pretty   pretey   pritee

cloathes   clothes   clowthes

moov   muve   move

Now have a look at these words.
Can you rewrite them with the correct spelling?

You can look back through this book for tips if you're stuck.

tryd _____

naym _____

chyldren _____

improov _____

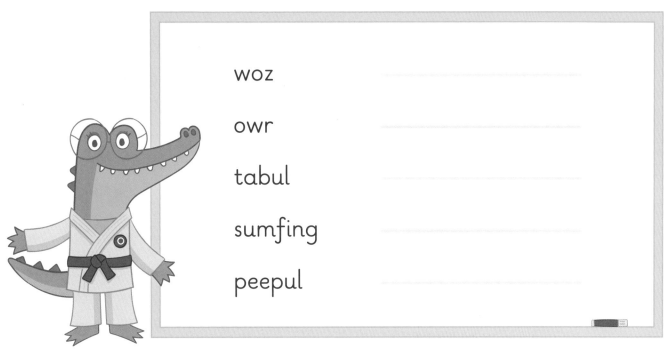

woz _____

owr _____

tabul _____

sumfing _____

peepul _____

frend _____

howse _____

fink _____

beecoz _____

sed _____

Answers

Pages 4–5
Letters games
Find the vowels
Ali
Tao
Olivia
Noah
Zara
Nia

Missing vowels

milk   sandwich
jump   lunchbox
sandpit   spoon
windmill   tree
pond   swing

Vowel swap
bell: ball, bull, bill; bond: bind, bend, band;
sock: sick, sack, suck

Mix and match the sounds

star   monkey
frog   clown
train
carrot

Pages 6–7
Tidy digraphs
bow   fork
chair   coins
book   towel
cars   boat
brush   clothes
pillow   train
toy   sloth
green

Pages 8–9
Digraph disco
Do the digraph dance
Olivia's dancing path goes through the words:
today, playing, holiday, maybe
Ali's dancing path goes through the words:
cloud, about, mouse
Zara's dancing path goes through the words:
enjoy, toy, annoying, joyful
Doubling up
tie, magpie, lie
feast, least, beast, east
girl, shirt, whirl, third
blue, clue, true
draw, yawn, saw, dawn, straw, fawn
new, grew
mangoes, toe

Pages 10–11
Digraphs and trigraphs
Split digraphs
time, cubes, shake, quite, broke, cone, ice,
cupcakes, bake, decorate, plate, rose, flake
Trigraphs

igh: knight, light, night
ear: ear, beard, tear
air: chair, hair, fairy
ure: manure, cure, secure

Pages 12–13
Words with rhythm
Clapping out words
recorder: 3, drum: 1, singing: 2, music: 2,
instrument: 3, rattle: 2, violin: 3, trumpet: 2,
horn: 1, piano: 3
Tidy syllables
1 syllable: mug, shoe, toy, glue, book
2 syllables: notebook, pencil, lunchbox, scissors
3 syllables: basketball, sharpener
More than 3 syllables: calculator

Pages 14–15
Same but different
Homophone snap
blue – blew; knight – night; brake – break;
flour – flower; hair – hare; sea – see;
bear – bare
The playscript
meet, missed, where, sea, there, witch, know,
right

Pages 16–17
Flower-sound families
Red: gain, explain, today, same
Green: speak, leak, peek, piece
Purple: boat, slow, throw, toe
Yellow: fly, high, sky, tide
Orange: blue, tube, new, moon
Blue: shout, how, trowel, shower

Pages 18–19
Sneaky spellings
Silent letters
Circled silent letters:

autumn   whale
answer   ghost
island   scissors
comb

Sounds like

tabul – table   sed – said   haz – has
whith – with   luv – love   tryd – tried
shoogar – sugar

Looks like
house, grass, friends, eye, father

Pages 20–21
Gone fishing
nk: drink, think, stinking, thanks, pink, monkey,
link
tion: education, subtraction, nation,
competition, addition
New endings
ca: catch, cage, cadge
swi: switch
fe: fetch
ske: sketch
bri: bridge
ba: batch, badge
fu: fudge
e: edge, etch
Home time
hudge, lege, chardge

Pages 22–23
Forest plurals
Collecting objects
cans, feathers, **crisp packets**, twigs,
plastic bags, pine cones, **sweet wrappers**,
acorns, **caps**, mushrooms, **bottles**
Funny plurals
blankets, torches, glasses, flags, lunchboxes,
robins, apples, benches, umbrellas

Pages 24–25
Practising prefixes
unhappy, unload, unzip, untidy, unwell, undo,
unfair, unsafe

Pages 26–27
Suffix games
-ment, -ness, -less and -ful
-ment: movement, pavement, agreement
-ness: fitness, illness, goodness
-less: endless, fearless, useless
-ful: careful, joyful, wonderful
-ly and -ing
-ly: quickly, fairly, rarely
-ing: playing, baking, jumping
-er and -est
fast, faster, fastest
slow, slower, slowest
small, smaller, smallest
tall, taller, tallest

Pages 28–29
Collecting words
birthday, paintbrush, milkshake, dragonfly,
playground
Sticking words back together
butterfly, skateboard, spaceship, popcorn,
rainbow

Pages 30–31
Spelling champion!
fast, water, money
thanks, school, you
pretty, clothes, move
tried, name, children, improve
was, our, table, something, people
friend, house, think, because, said